THIS BOOK
BELONGS TO

BIG JOKES BOOK
BOOK
CHRISTMAS!

WHO TELLS THE BEST CHRISTMAS JOKES?

REINDEER. THEY SLEIGH EVERY TIME

WHERE WOULD A REINDEER GO TO FIND HER LOST TAIL?

"RE-TAIL" STORE

KNOCK, KNOCK!
WHO'S THERE?
JUSTIN.
JUSTIN WHO?
JUSTIN TIME FOR CHRISTMAS
COOKIES!

MY FRIEND JUST WON THE
TALLEST CHRISTMAS TREE
COMPETITION.

I THOUGHT TO MYSELF,
"HOW CAN YOU TOP THAT?"

WHAT WOULD YOU CALL
AN ELF WHO JUST HAS
WON THE LOTTERY?

WELFY

KNOCK, KNOCK!
WHO'S THERE?
DONUT. DONUT WHO?
DONUT OPEN TIL CHRISTMAS!

DID YOU KNOW THAT SANTA ACTUALLY ONLY HAD TWO REINDEER?

RUDOLPH AND OLIVE (THE OTHER REINDEER)

WHAT WOULD YOU CALL THE TWELFTH ELF THAT COMES TO HELP OTHER 11 ELVES IN THE WORKSHOP?

THE TWELF

WHAT MONTH DOES A CHRISTMAS TREE HATE THE MOST?

SEP-TIMBER!

THE ONLY CHRISTMAS PRESENT THAT I GOT THIS YEAR WAS A DECK OF STICKY PLAYING CARDS

I FIND THAT VERY HARD TO DEAL WITH

WHAT DID ONE
CHRISTMAS TREE
SAY TO ANOTHER?

LIGHTEN UP!

ELVES USE WHAT
KIND OF MONEY?

JINGLE BILLS!

WHAT DO YOU CALL A SNOWMAN WITH A SIX PACK?

AN ABDOMINAL SNOWMAN

HOW DID ELVES CLIMBED UP TO THE TOP OF SANTA'S CASTLE?

USING AN "ELF"-EVATOR.

WHAT DO YOU GET WHEN YOU MIX A CHRISTMAS TREE AND AN IPAD?

A PINEAPPLE!

WHY DID MRS. CLAUS INSIST SANTA TAKE AN UMBRELLA?

"BECAUSE OF THE RAIN, DEAR."

WHERE DOES A
SNOWMAN KEEP HIS
MONEY?

IN A SNOW BANK

WHAT DID THE BEAVER
SAY TO THE CHRISTMAS
TREE?

NICE GNAWING YOU!

WHO IS SANTA'S
FAVOURITE ACTOR?

WILLEM DAFOE-HO-HO

WHY DOES IT TAKE
LONGER TO BUILD A
BLONDE SNOWMAN?

YOU HAVE TO HOLLOW
OUT ITS HEAD FIRST

WHO IS A CHRISTMAS TREE'S FAVORITE SINGER?

SPRUCE SPRINGSTEEN

WHERE DOES SANTA CLAUS GO SWIMMING?

THE NORTH POOL

HOW ONE SNOWMAN GREETS THE OTHER ONE?

ICE TO MEET YOU

WHAT DO YOU CALL A SNOWMAN ON ROLLERBLADES?

A SNOWMOBILE

WHAT HAPPENS IF YOU
EAT CHRISTMAS
DECORATIONS?

YOU GET TINSEL-IT IS

HOW DID THE REINDEER
LEARN TO PLAY PIANO?

HE WAS ELF-TAUGHT

WHAT DO HUNGRY SNOWMEN PUT ON THEIR ICE-BURGERS?

CHILLY SAUCE!

WHY ARE CHRISTMAS TREES SO BAD AT KNITTING?

THEY HAVE TOO MANY NEEDLES

WIFE: I REGRET GETTING YOU THAT BLENDER FOR CHRISTMAS.

ME: *SIPPING TOAST* WHY?

HOW DO SHEEP IN MEXICO GREET MERRY CHRISTMAS?

FLEECE NAVIDAD!

WHAT DO YOU CALL CUTTING DOWN A CHRISTMAS TREE?

CHRISTMAS CHOPPING!

WHAT'S A REINDEER'S FAVOURITE SINGER?

BEYONSLEIGH

HOW TO CATS GREET EACH OTHER AT CHRISTMAS?

"A FURRY MERRY CHRISTMAS & HAPPY MEW YEAR!"

WHY ARE CHRISTMAS TREES SO FOND OF THE PAST?

BECAUSE THE PRESENT'S BENEATH THEM

WHAT DID THE THIRD WISE SALESMAN SAY AFTER HIS FRIENDS HAD ALREADY PRESENTED GOLD AND FRANKINCENSE?

BUT WAIT – THERE'S MYRRH!

HOW DO YOU GREET AN IDIOT ON BOXING DAY?

TELL HIM A JOKE ON CHRISTMAS EVE!

WHAT IS A CHRISTMAS TREE'S FAVORITE CANDY?

ORNA-MINTS!

WHY IS EVERYONE THIRSTY AT THE NORTH POLE?

NO WELL

WHAT KIND OF MUSIC DOES ELVES LIKE BEST WHEN HE HAS TO GREET?

"WRAP" MUSIC!

WHY DID SANTA CLAUS GET A PARKING TICKET ON CHRISTMAS EVE?

HE LEFT HIS SLEIGH IN A SNOW PARKING ZONE

I BOUGHT MY SON A FRIDGE FOR CHRISTMAS

I CAN'T WAIT TO SEE HIS FACE LIGHT UP WHEN HE OPENS IT

HOW CAN YOU KEEP SANTA BUSY IN THE CHRISTMAS PARTY?

ASK HIM TO TAKE CARE OF YOUR PLANTS.

WHAT DO YOU GET IF YOU CROSS SANTA WITH A DUCK?

A CHRISTMAS QUACKER

WHAT DID FROSTY'S GIRLFRIEND GIVE HIM WHEN SHE WAS MAD AT HIM?

THE COLD SHOULDER

WHOSE CHRISTMAS PARTIES ARE FULL OF SCREAMS?

DRACULA'S

WHAT GOES "OH, OH, OH"?

SANTA WALKING BACKWARDS!

WHO DOES SANTA CALL
WHEN HIS SLEIGH
BREAKS DOWN?

THE ABOMINABLE
TOWMAN

WHAT YOU CAN CALL A
POLAR BEAR WHICH
WEARS EAR MUFFS?

ANYTHING YOU WANT.
HE CAN'T HEAR YOU!

WHAT DO YOU CALL A BROKE SANTA CLAUS?

SAINT-NICKEL-LESS

WHAT DO YOU CALL PEOPLE WHO ARE AFRAID OF SANTA?

CLAUSTROPHOBIC

WHAT'S A SNOWMAN'S FAVORITE MEXICAN FOOD?

BRRRRRR-ITOS!

HOW MUCH DID SANTA PAY FOR HIS SLEIGH?

NOTHING, IT WAS ON THE HOUSE!

WHAT DO YOU CALL AN OLD SNOWMAN?

WATER

A GUY BOUGHT HIS WIFE A BEAUTIFUL DIAMOND RING FOR CHRISTMAS. AFTER HEARING ABOUT THIS EXTRAVAGANT GIFT, A FRIEND OF HIS SAID,

"I THOUGHT SHE WANTED ONE OF THOSE SPORTY FOUR-WHEEL-DRIVE VEHICLES."

"SHE DID," HE REPLIED. "BUT WHERE WAS I GOING TO FIND A FAKE JEEP?"

WHY DOES SANTA ALWAYS ENTER THROUGH THE CHIMNEY?

BECAUSE IT SOOTS HIM

I GOT A UNIVERSAL REMOTE CONTROL FOR CHRISTMAS

THIS CHANGES EVERYTHING

ESKIMOS SING WHAT
DURING THEIR DINNER?

"WHALE MEAT AGAIN,
DON'T KNOW WHERE,
DON'T KNOW WHEN"!

WHAT WAS SANTA'S
FAVORITE SUBJECT
IN SCHOOL?

CHEMIS-TREE!

WHY DID THE TURKEY
JOIN THE ROCK BAND?

BECAUSE IT HAD
DRUMSTICKS

HOW DOES GOOD KING
WENCESLAS LIKE HIS
PIZZAS?

DEEP PAN, CRISP AND
EVEN!

HOW DO YOU KNOW WHEN SANTA'S AROUND?

YOU CAN ALWAYS SENSE HIS PRESENTS

HOW DO THE ELVES CLEAN SANTA'S SLEIGH ON THE DAY AFTER CHRISTMAS?

THEY USE SANTA-TIZER

WHAT KIND OF MOTORBIKE DOES SANTA RIDE?

A HOLLY DAVIDSON

WHAT BEST YOU CAN PUT INTO THE CHRISTMAS CAKE?

YOUR TEETH

WHAT IS SANTA'S FAVORITE KIND OF CANDY?

JOLLY RANCHERS

HOW DID MARY AND JOSEPH KNOW THAT JESUS WAS 8 LB 2 OZ WHEN HE WAS BORN?

THEY HAD A WEIGH IN A MANGER

DO I HAVE PERMISSION TO EAT A DOG THIS CHRISTMAS?

ONLY TURKEY LIKE EVERYONE ELSE

WHAT DO SNOWMEN EAT FOR BREAKFAST?

ICE CRISPIES

THE CHRISTMAS JUMPER MY KIDS GAVE ME LAST YEAR KEPT PICKING UP STATIC ELECTRICITY

I TOOK IT BACK AND EXCHANGED IT FOR ANOTHER ONE – FREE OF CHARGE

WHY DID THE KIDS START EATING THE PUZZLE ON CHRISTMAS?

BECAUSE THEIR UNCLE SAID THAT IT WAS A PIECE OF CAKE!

WHAT DID THE GINGERBREAD MAN PUT ON HIS BED?

A COOKIE SHEET!

DID YOU HEAR ABOUT THE MAN WHO STOLE AN ADVENT CALENDAR?

HE GOT 25 DAYS

WHAT A BIG CANDLE SAYS TO A SMALL CANDLE ON A CHRISTMAS EVE?

I AM GOING OUT FOR DINNER TONIGHT.

WHAT'S THE DIFFERENCE BETWEEN THE CHRISTMAS ALPHABET AND THE ORDINARY ALPHABET?

THE CHRISTMAS ALPHABET HAS NOEL

WHY DID NO-ONE BID
FOR RUDOLPH AND
BLITZEN ON EBAY?

BECAUSE THEY WERE
TWO DEER

A SNOWMAN LOSES
WEIGHT IN WHAT WAY?

HE WAITS FOR THE
WEATHER TO GET
WARMER!

WHAT DO GRAPES SING AT CHRISTMAS?

TIS THE SEASON TO BE JELLY

WHAT DO YOU GET WHEN YOU CROSS A SNOWMAN WITH A VAMPIRE?

FROSTBITE

WHAT'S A GOOD CHRISTMAS TIP?

NEVER CATCH SNOWFLAKES WITH YOUR TONGUE UNTIL ALL THE BIRDS HAVE GONE SOUTH FOR THE WINTER

WHAT DO YOU CALL AN OBNOXIOUS REINDEER?

RUDE-OLPH

WHY DID THE RED-NOSED REINDEER HELP THE OLD LADY CROSS THE ROAD?

IT WOULD HAVE BEEN RUDOLPH HIM NOT TO

THREE MEN DIE IN A CAR ACCIDENT ON CHRISTMAS EVE. THEY ALL FIND THEMSELVES AT THE PEARLY GATES WAITING TO ENTER HEAVEN. ON ENTERING THEY MUST PRESENT SOMETHING RELATING TO OR ASSOCIATED WITH CHRISTMAS. THE FIRST MAN SEARCHES HIS POCKET, AND FINDS SOME MISTLETOE, SO HE IS ALLOWED IN. THE SECOND MAN PRESENTS A CRACKER, SO HE IS ALSO ALLOWED IN. THE THIRD MAN PULLS OUT A PAIR OF STOCKINGS. CONFUSED AT THIS LAST GESTURE, ST PETER ASKS, 'HOW DO THESE REPRESENT CHRISTMAS?

ANSWER: 'THEY'RE CAROL'S.'

WHAT DO SANTA'S ELVES LEARN IN SCHOOL?

THE ELF-ABET

WHAT IS SANTA'S FAVOURITE KIND OF PIZZA?

ONE THAT'S DEEP-PAN, CRISP AND EVEN

THE BERMUDA TRIANGLE GOT TIRED OF WARM WEATHER. IT MOVED TO FINLAND. NOW SANTA CLAUS IS MISSING

WHAT HAPPENS IF YOU EAT CHRISTMAS DECORATIONS?

YOU GET TINSEL-IT IS

WHAT DOES SANTA DO WHEN HIS ELVES MISBEHAVE?

HE GIVES THEM THE SACK

WHAT COULD BE A PERFECT GIFT FOR THE STATION MASTER DURING CHRISTMAS?

PLATFORM SHOES

WHAT'S THE ABSOLUTE BEST CHRISTMAS PRESENT?

A BROKEN DRUM — YOU CAN'T BEAT IT!

I GOT A CHRISTMAS CARD FULL OF RICE IN THE POST TODAY.

I THINK IT WAS FROM MY UNCLE BEN

WHY THE CHRISTMAS TREE CAN'T STAND UP?

IT DOESN'T HAVE LEGS

WHAT DID ADAM SAY TO HIS WIFE ON THE DAY BEFORE CHRISTMAS?

IT'S CHRISTMAS, EVE!

WHERE DO SANTA'S REINDEER STOP FOR COFFEE?

STAR-BUCKS!

WHY ARE CHRISTMAS TREES SO BAD AT SEWING?

THEY'RE ALWAYS DROPPING THEIR NEEDLES

DIFFERENTIATE BETWEEN CHRISTMAS ALPHABET AND ORDINARY ALPHABET?

THE CHRISTMAS ALPHABET HAS NOEL

WHY DID SANTA HAVE TO GO TO THE HOSPITAL?

BECAUSE OF HIS POOR ELF

WHAT IS THE POPULAR CAROL IN DESERT?

CAMEL YE FAITHFUL

I HAVE THIS INCREDIBLE ABILITY TO PREDICT WHAT'S INSIDE A WRAPPED PRESENT

IT'S A GIFT

WHAT DO YOU CALL A
FROG HANGING FROM
THE CEILING?

MISTLETOAD

WHAT IS ONE OF THE BEST
CHRISTMAS PRESENTS THAT
YOU CAN GIVE AND
RECEIVE?A BROKEN DRUM

WHY?

BECAUSE YOU CAN'T BEAT
IT!

One last thing...

We would love to hear your feedback about this book!

If you enjoyed this book or found it useful, we would be very grateful if you posted a short review on Amazon. Your support does make a difference and we read every review personally.

If you would like to leave a review, all you need to do is click the review link on this book's page on Amazon

Thank you for your support!

www.enjoydiscovering.net.pl

Made in the USA
Las Vegas, NV
13 December 2021

37513989R00031